Sunlight through the Trees and Other Poems

Sunlight through the Trees and Other Poems

Kristi Bishop

RESOURCE *Publications* • Eugene, Oregon

SUNLIGHT THROUGH THE TREES AND OTHER POEMS

Resource Publications
An Imprint of Wipf and Stock Publishers
199 W. 8th Ave., Suite 3
Eugene, OR 97401

www.wipfandstock.com

PAPERBACK ISBN: 978-1-7252-9049-5
HARDCOVER ISBN: 978-1-7252-9050-1
EBOOK ISBN: 978-1-7252-9051-8

June 15, 2021

For my mom

Contents

Preface

More than anything else, my observations within the world of nature inspire me to write poetry. I may be looking across wide open fields as I drive, walking in quiet woodlands, or weeding my flower gardens, when an idea or phrase enters my mind to later become a rhyming verse. And just when I think that maybe this flow of ideas has ceased, one more revelation touches my heart, and I find myself writing yet again. I know deep in my soul that these thoughts turned poems are gifts from God, an answer to a silent prayer for connections with him as I go about my days.

My creativity also stems from thinking about God, especially reflecting on his love and goodness or expressing gratitude for his intimate friendship and miraculous salvation. The anticipation of heaven, when I will walk with God and talk to him face to face, is often conveyed as I write. Other poems describe my goals of loving and serving the people who cross my path.

Nature and God are frequently intertwined when I put pen to paper as they are difficult, if not impossible, for me to separate. I see every plant, tree, animal, raindrop, and sunbeam as a present to me personally from the Creator, and I am moved to give him my heart. These poems essentially are prayers to the one who gave them to me in the first place, and I can't help but return them to their rightful owner. In turn, it is my privilege and joy to share them with you, my reader, as well.

Acknowledgements

I WOULD LIKE TO thank my sister, Tina Frist Smith, for always believing in me, and for her invaluable work as my editor. Only with her help was I able to adequately communicate the inspiration behind each poem and elaborate on its contents. Tina is a gifted and dedicated writer, and she gave the gifts of her time and expertise freely and lovingly. She also assisted me with many other elements involved in getting this book ready to publish.

I am also indebted to my husband, Roddy, for his love and support during more than three decades of marriage and particularly during the process of bringing this project to completion. His technical assistance, role as a sounding board, and encouragement when I felt overwhelmed and unsure were genuine contributions to this volume of poetry.

Most of all, I am grateful to God, who put these poems in my heart and continues to inspire me every day with the beauty and wonder found in nature and the joy and peace flowing from his divine grace and love.

The Brush of Angels' Wings

The softest brush of angels' wings
I thought I felt one day,
As I paused for just a moment
Before hurrying on my way.

I stopped to feel the sunshine,
And hear the sweet birds sing,
And think about the blessings,
That each day always brings.

I reveled in the cool breeze
Blowing softly on my face,
I thought about the vastness
And the mystery of space.

I thanked God for the beauty,
In all the world around,
For mountains and for oceans,
For sight and smell and sound.

I heard celestial music,
And God's voice seemed to say,
"Heaven's very close to you
And touching you today."

When I Was a Child

I GREW UP IN a house located on 16 wooden acres and as a youngster spent many hours exploring this outdoor wonderland. Often I would set out alone to revel in the exquisite natural beauty of the property. Down at the creek, I would unclog the flow of water jammed with leaves. I would identify wildflowers and trees, observing the timeless changing of the seasons. During my times in the woods, I always felt joyful and especially close to the Creator, almost expecting to see him around the next corner. I firmly believe he walked beside me as I climbed the sloping hills and wandered the old paths. I treasure those precious times in my heart and often wish I could go back to that period of innocence and openness, when the veil between heaven and earth seemed very thin.

When I was a child I would go to the woods —
I'd walk the short path to the creek,
Under the trees, a canopy green,
With the sunlight caressing my cheek.

There in the woods, though all alone,
I wouldn't good company lack,
The trees would whisper their secrets to me,
And my thoughts would answer them back.

The angels were there, and God himself —
I'd commune with Creator Grand,

I'd crunch through the leaves and over the logs,
And feel so in touch with the land.

I'd sit by the creek, and dangle my legs
Over water that bubbled and flowed,
I might remove shoes and wade for a while —
The smell of damp earth in my nose.

So at peace with our God, and with myself, too,
As on through the woods I would roam,
And then climb the hill graced with flowers bright,
And reluctantly turn my steps home.

I'd love to go back to those times in the woods,
When heaven came down close to me,
When I talked to God and heard his small voice,
In his nature so happy and free.

After the Rain

What a treat for the senses is the glistening outdoors following a cloudburst! Dripping foliage and twittering birds are the only sounds to be heard in the stillness, and the moist air feels fresh and clean on skin. The wet ground emits an earthy scent, and all nature seems to sparkle. There's a pervasive feeling of renewal that inspires me to ask God to revive my heart, wash me clean, and start a spring of soulful joy bubbling up. The dampened nature reminds me again to look to the Creator for abundant life.

After the rain is a lovely time,
When all nature is washed anew,
The birds come back out from their sheltering spots,
And the beautiful Mourning Doves coo.

The smell of the earth, so wonderfully damp,
I breathe deeply in, and I see
The glistening leaves, dripping water down
From my towering, friendly oak tree.

I hear distant thunder as the rain moves away,
To refresh some other dry place,
I touch the wet grass, so sparkling clean,
And I feel the moist air on my face.

The rain has left puddles, here and there,
For the robins to vigorously bathe in.

The creek is now running and bubbling free —
The floating leaves swirling paths paving.

After the rain, I relish the time
That I spend in this fresh outdoor scene,
The smells, sights and textures I aptly enjoy,
Now that the earth is washed clean.

The Song of a Bird

Birds are one of my favorite animals for a variety of reasons. I love their colors, antics, chirps, and songs. I am fascinated by their nests, behavior, and migratory patterns. Even my home décor reflects my love of birds, with their images in wall art, on a lamp, even on my napkin holder. Bird songs are another wonderful aspect of these creatures. I recognize a few songs as belonging to specific birds, and I find great satisfaction in identifying fowl in this way. There's nothing quite like watching a bird sing for all it's worth and marveling at the beautiful sounds produced by such a small being. Bird songs are consistently cheerful and soothing to me, never failing to bring a smile to my face and joy to my heart.

The song of a bird is a wonderful thing,
Whether whistled or whispered low,
What goes through the mind of a bird as it sings
Is something God only can know.

The song of a bird always brightens the day,
In the morning right up to the night,
Sometimes one might think a song never will end,
As the bird sings with all of its might.

You might hear the song of a bird in the rain,
Or even before the sun's rising,
You might hear it far away or close to home,
And its motive I'll leave to surmising.

But surely the birds must have joy in their hearts,
And praise to our God up above,
Their songs are most certainly ways that he shows us
The fathomless depths of his love.

So the next time you hear a melody sweet,
Sung by a most-lowly bird,
Look up to our loving Creator-God,
And give thanks for what you have heard.

At the Seashore

Oh, how I love a vacation at the beach! I feel a million miles from home and all my responsibilities and problems. At the beach there is no laundry to wash or food to cook, no job to get to each morning. I can truly relax and "get away from it all." I spend my day down at the water's edge in a chair under an umbrella. There I read and nap, write, dream, and people-watch. Each beach experience is a gift from the Creator, who fashioned such a delightful environment for me. The sights and sounds provided by the ocean are ideally conducive to soul-searching and planning for change, and by the end of each stay I feel rested and centered, ready to take up my duties and challenges at home once again.

The endless sky meets the arrow-straight, deep blue line abruptly, the colors of sky and water clashing together beautifully. White clouds appear to be frozen, silently suspended against their will between water and haze.

The azure and green water undulates all the way to the horizon.

The waves are relentless, one after the other, each coming nearer and nearer and rising up, up, up, before reluctantly breaking in a hissing, foaming white froth that travels as far as it can before disappearing forever, never to return. I am powerless against the force of the moving, green liquid. It tries to push me, and pull me with its strength, and seems to laugh at my helplessness. I stumble to shore, struggling through the sinking, wet sand and then up through the dry but shifting grains.

Under my umbrella I am sheltered and safe from the rays of the blazing orb that arcs slowly, effortlessly, high above, warming and nurturing all below. The breeze, cool and reviving, caresses me and soothes my anxious mind. The sea air is warm and pungent in my nose, and tastes faintly salty on my tongue. The roar of the waves cannot be silenced; day and night it boasts of power and constancy, yet somehow lulls and quiets my very being.

Time seems to stand still, and this place feels like a healing wave washing over me. I feel cleansed and better for all that I experience in this sacred space, a slice of the earth that for now I possess and breathe.

Colors of Nature

WRITTEN IN 1985 WHILE I was still in high school, this is my oldest published poem, a precious piece of evidence of my love for nature beginning when I was young. I can still feel the desire that prompted this writing — the longing to somehow experience God's second book even more deeply and to gather the beauty found to myself and never let it go. Even with aging and jading brought by time and with innocence lost, I sense that same stirring at times now, a desperate need to experience the natural world in a way like never before. It's an aching loneliness rooted in the eagerness to experience not just nature but God himself. That's what the earth does: it draws us to God and reveals God to us, if we will only let it.

I wish that I could hold the blue
That God put in the sky,
And put it in a picture
Or a sweater that is mine.

I wish that I could take the reds
And greens of autumn's tree,
And save them for a rainy day
To cheer and uplift me.

I wish that I could take the bronze
Of sun, the molten gold,
And make it into something I
Could feel and keep and hold.

I wish that I could take the mauve
Of the thistle's striking flower,
And keep it in a vase or jar
To brighten every hour.

Although I wish for all these things,
These colors are mine to see,
And their beauty leads me to praise him
Who in love made them for me.

The Greatness of God

HAVE YOU EVER FELT overwhelmed by the greatness of God? At times, all that he is and all that he does washes over me in a crashing wave, and my heart seems to almost burst. I believe these moments are truly a rare kind of gift, these times when God breaks through all my negativity, doubt, and discouragement, and gives me a vision of himself. Miracle moments, I like to call them. Moments I hope will happen more frequently as I grow closer to him. It was during one of those miracles that I wrote this poem, which seemed to come out of nowhere, just like that moment.

The greatness of God can be hard to describe,
It's too big to hold in my hand,
I can only attempt to convey all he is,
Whose great works outnumber the sand.

His power and might are easily seen,
From sunrise till close of the day,
And even at night his awesomeness shows
As the stars shine and come out to play.

All his creation must burst forth with praise
As soon as they come into being,
The trees of the forest, the oceans, and mounts,
And the bright little birds ever singing.

The worlds as they spin, to the atoms so small,
All tell of how great our God is,
He made all the animals, their every detail,
Their clever designs are all his.

And how God can know each and every man's name
Is beyond what my small brain can think,
And how when he comes, we will know him at once,
And be changed in one tiny eye's wink.

And then, Oh, amazement! What infinite love
Caused such a great God to give,
All of himself in the form of his son,
So a wretch such as I might then live.

Taking my place in an unfair charade,
And giving his robe for some dice,
Stretching his hands out he embraced the world,
And then paid the ultimate price.

His love is what makes God the greatest of all,
His love is what sets him apart,
His love is what draws me and binds me to him,
And prompts me to give him my heart.

Each Day Is One Day Closer

WHAT IS A DAY? Just a 24-hour period that we live in, count on calendars, and obey as a constraint. It is an odd and varied entity, this concept. Days blend together like water colors on a canvas, sorted out roughly into weeks and weekends, holidays and vacations. Some days we refer to as "good," others as "bad." But maybe we are going about this "day thing" all wrong. Maybe we should count down our days instead of counting them up, measuring each by how close we are to the end of days and the end of time, when an infinitely more glorious way of living will be ours to share forever with those we love and with the one who has loved us every day of our lives.

Each day is one day closer
To that day I'm dreaming of,
That glorious day when I will see
My heavenly home above.

I'll see my precious Savior
And the loved ones I have lost,
I'll thank my dear Redeemer,
For having paid the cost

I should have had to pay. Instead,
I'm free and crystal clear,
Of that awful sinful burden,
And all the pain and tears

I've suffered while down here on earth,
But never will up there,
Only peace and happiness
Will be mine with him to share.

And all my friends and family,
Right by the crystal sea,
I'll find and then embrace
And live with for eternity.

God Repeats Himself

THIS POEM WAS INSPIRED by a quote, the exact wording since forgotten, that referred to nature repeating itself. This concept resonated deeply with me. Even as a devoted lover of the great outdoors, I had not thought much about the reiteration in nature — not tedious or dull repetition, but beautiful refrains in timeless songs of life. As I composed, several soothing, rhythmic aspects came to mind, and I realized that God is the author and sustainer of these rhythms. He repeats himself because he knows we need the reassurance and comfort that the repetition provides. This repeating is another reminder from God that he will never change or ever cease to love and care for us.

Have you noticed God repeats himself
In nature and in life,
In how evening turns to morning,
And day fades into night?

I think it's oft' to comfort us
And maybe help us see,
The rhythm and the staying
Of his love for you and me.

For wouldn't it be odd
If an older man turned younger?
Or instead of giving us more strength
Eating food just caused more hunger?

Instead life is a cycle,
From birth to age to death,
Our growth follows a pattern,
That starts with our first breath.

I'm glad that when we're mourning,
We move from stage to stage,
We finally find acceptance
Through denial, tears and rage.

Just think, how our world's water,
Flows from high to low,
When rain comes down in torrents,
We know which way it goes —

From ground to stream to river,
Then to the ocean vast,
Then mists rise upward to the clouds
Which hold their stores steadfast

Until it's time to rain again.
The cycle never ends,
And neither does God's love and care
And strength he daily sends.

Just like the cycling water,
God's gifts will never cease,
They flow from him each morning,
To bring us hope and peace.

In all these things God shows us,
He always is the same,
He's always there, no matter where
or when we call his name.

As constant as the sun and moon
That in their courses go,
The fountain never will dry up
From whence his mercies flow.

The Lining of Those Clouds

"There's always a silver lining" has long been one of my favorite expressions, and I find myself using it regularly. It is a very true statement, fitting of many situations, and a great attitude for life. Surprisingly, that expression did not directly inspire this poem. The thoughts instead came to me on one of my morning walks. It was a sunny start to the day, but for a moment the rays were just barely obscured by a cloud. The sun illuminated the edge of the cloud, causing it to glow brilliantly silver. It was indescribably beautiful. Oh, for the faith to keep this scene in my mind when life's challenges arise, and the clouds hang heavy and low! I'll forever hold the vision of that beautiful silver lining in my heart to serve me well whenever I cannot see the sunshine.

I know the storm is raging
And the rain is pouring down,
But I wish that you could only see
The lining of those clouds.

It's silver and it's glowing
Far above the storm right now,
You'd never know down here below,
The brilliant lining of those clouds.

It's hard to just imagine
That those harsh winds cannot last,

Very soon the sun will come out
And the sadness will be past.

There's a certain time for weeping
But there's also time to sing,
Although your heart is heavy now
It surely will take wings

And soar to heights it's never been —
You'll make the eagle proud,
And shine so bright, yes, brighter than
The silver lining of those clouds.

God's Canvas

THE EVER-CHANGING BEAUTY OF the sky delights me. Whether bright or gloomy, I enjoy the sky's enormity and grandeur. Sometimes it is high and endless, a great bowl of blue over the landscape. Other times the thick, gray clouds form a much closer, intimate ceiling. I love to watch birds flit about in the sky or soar effortlessly on mysterious air currents. Sunsets and sunrises yield gorgeous patterns of color that surround the glowing ball of sun, greeting the new day or ushering in the night. What a wonderful aspect of nature, and one easily taken for granted. For pleasure and inspiration, all we need to do is look up.

The sky is a canvas
God uses each day,
To paint many pictures
In various ways.

He may paint it brilliantly,
Beautifully blue,
And dot it with clouds
And birds many or few.

There may be great blankets
Of gray clouds that pour,
Out the fresh rain
'til the earth wants no more.

God may use the sky
To show off his great power,
With streaks of bright lightening
That sound through the hours.

He might light the night sky
With millions of stars,
Or showcase a moon
That seems close, though it's far.

God may grace with colors
The sky at the dawn —
A feast for our eyes
'til it fades, and is gone.

Like an artist he works
To create for our eyes,
These gifts every day
We can find in the skies.

He Didn't Have To

IT IS EASY TO take the beautiful world of nature for granted. The trees and sky, wildlife and foliage that we live and breathe in each day can become so familiar that we no longer see them. When nature's beauty becomes lost to us, we lose out on much more than these gifts to our senses — we miss poignant messages of love from God. Long ago his creative mind and heart brought this world and all its beauty into being, and his power continues to sustain it. Why? For us, his dearly loved children. Until he can live with us face to face, nature is one of God's most important ways of speaking messages of comfort, love, and instruction. Each day we have the privilege of hearing these messages, if our hearts remain open, thankful, and trusting.

God didn't have to make so many kinds of birds to see,
He didn't have to form the graceful branches of each tree.
He surely could've made the sky a dark and dreary hue,
Instead he made it shine out with a vibrant, perfect blue.

The golden sun could still come up each morning when we rise,
without the brilliant strokes of paint that often grace the skies.
He didn't have to shape the earth in forms so smooth and grand,
He didn't have to make the ocean waves foam on the sand.

He didn't have to take the time to form each lovely flower,
He could have chosen not to share his great creative power.
God didn't have to give us all this beauty that we see,
but he knew that it would help to show his love for you and me.

I Go Walking in the Morning

WALKING IS DEFINITELY MY preferred type of exercise, and first thing in the morning is my favorite time to walk. Getting outside and moving is such a positive way to begin the day. Sometimes walking feels more like a prayer to me than an exercise. I feel God's presence keenly, and during these times it seems the wonders of nature were put in place specifically for me. God's beauty, power, and love on display all have a tendency to wash over me as I walk along. I return home feeling refreshed physically, mentally, and spiritually.

I go walking in the morning,
I go 'most every day,
I like to feel the cool air
And the sunshine on my face.

The grass is bright with diamonds,
And wet with sparkling dew,
Just like the Father's mercies
Every morning fresh and new.

I might just see a rabbit
Standing still and tall and gray,
And then as I get closer
Watch his white tail hop away.

I might walk to the rushing creek

And see the shining water,
And think about the living spring
That flows out from the Father.

I hear the distant cooing
Of the sweet and gentle doves,
And also hear God's whispers
In my ear of his great love.

God may place along my walking path
Some lovely flowers to share,
Or a golden tree or flitting bird
To show how much he cares.

The sky is blue above me
And the sun is shining bright,
They tell me of his wonder
Of his majesty and might.

I go walking in the morning,
I go 'most every day,
And God comes near to show his love,
All along my way.

The Names of God

I WAS MEDITATING ONE day on the many names of God that we find in the Bible — dozens of names — each speaking to a respective role and characteristic of an extremely complex and wonderful person. I kept thinking of more and more names, listing them in my mind, and decided to put some of these names into a poem. My creation doesn't do him or his names justice, but seeing all those names together in one place reminds me of his greatness. I am inspired to dedicate myself anew to trusting and loving our marvelous Father completely.

Our God is so big, and his greatness so grand,
He cannot have only one name,
And all of his names tell us more of his power,
And how he's forever the same.

Spirit that's holy, Father, and Son,
Make up the God that we love,
The trinity three, a trio complete,
That together make up the one.

Jesus, the Son, the Pearl of Great Price,
Became the Light of the World,
The Living Water, and Bread of Life,
While temptations at him were hurled.

He's our Good Shepherd, keeping his flock

Safe from the wolves ever roaming,
Our Savior, Messiah, his love is more vast
Than the deep and the vast ocean foaming.

Everlasting Father, Hiding Place true,
The Creator of all that we see,
Alpha, Omega, the First and the Last,
And Comforter when we should weep.

King of All Kings, and Lord of Lords,
Are titles most fit for our God,
He's Wonderful, Counselor, a Prince of Peace,
And the True Vine that grows without sod.

Cornerstone, Potter, and Great High Priest,
Interceding for me up above,
Redeemer, and Friend of Sinners all,
Savior, who died out of love.

So many wonderful, fitting names
For the one who is simply "I Am,"
I'll trust him and love him and watch as unfolds
His perfect and glorious plan.

On a Tree That You Made Grow

How ironic that Jesus came to love a world that largely rejected him, ultimately mistreating and killing him — the Creator unaccepted and unloved by his creation. Jesus's entire life was a paradox: as a child, learning the very scriptures that he had inspired; as a youth, he who winds and waves obeyed being obedient to his parents; as a young man, the adored of heaven humbly working in a dusty carpenter shop; during his ministry, the fountain of all wisdom questioned and harassed by the religious teachers of his day. Yet he endured it all, despising the shame, and sat down at the right hand of God after rising from the dead. And evermore he will reign in his rightful place with God. More than that, he invites us to reign with him, as the ceaseless ages roll. What an amazing mystery! Such great love will take an eternity to fathom.

On a hill that you created,
On a tree that you made grow,
By men whose breath you gave them
You were caused to suffer so.

You came to earth to bring men peace,
But they wanted only strife,
In the end betraying you
And taking your precious life.

Those loving hands you stretched out,
You willingly gave your all,

Your gentle voice was silenced,
Your pure tears ceased to fall.

But even in your lonely tomb
The hope you brought lived on,
You rose to life on that third day
To greet the glorious dawn.

Your life and death, your holy work,
Were all for ones like me,
To bring us love and joy and light,
And a home we'll someday see.

God's Thoughts

ALTHOUGH OUR HUMAN BRAINS cannot fathom God's thoughts, the Bible does give us a glimpse of what goes on in God's mind through its many stories, psalms, and letters. Nature also has much to tell us about God's character and his thoughts about us. The challenge to remember that his thoughts are higher than ours and always good toward us arises when we go through trials, which are certain and often. Life is simply a series of problems to be solved — once we resolve one trial or challenge, another comes to take its place. So remembering our place in God's mind as well as in relation to those heavenly thoughts is vitally important as we go through life. Such mindfulness will sustain us through the storms we are sure to face.

God's thoughts are much higher than our thoughts,
We can't always know what he's planned,
The way that he thinks is beyond us —
The small puny mind of mere man.

But some things in his mind we do know,
Like his great love for us and his plan,
To only give help and not harm us,
And give us what only he can.

Like a future so bright and so hopeful,
Salvation so sweet and so true,
His thoughts towards us always are loving,

He's thinking of all he can do

To hold us, uplift us, and bless us,
And guide us through storms that are rough,
He thinks of the ways he can hopefully,
Show us his love is enough.

So remember you always can trust him,
It takes faith on our part, yes, that's true,
To know God's thoughts rise far above us,
Above earth and the heavens, too.

He's Just Glad We Came

NOTHING WE BRING TO God surprises or annoys him. We are incapable of disappointing him with our presence; he simply longs to spend time with us, to listen to us, to hold us. We never face judgment or apathy with God, and he will never shame or belittle us. Why then do we sometimes hesitate to bring him our sorrows, joys, and problems? He is the ultimate listener, the dearest friend, the epitome of goodness, kindness, and love. Let's go to him without holding back. We have nothing to fear and everything to gain by coming to God.

When we come to God with grief and doubt,
Even bitterness and blame,
He never turns away from us,
He's just glad we came.

When we come bowed down with guilt so black
Our hearts are full of shame,
He lovingly forgives us,
And he's so glad we came.

When in love we come to God
With our heart's light aflame,
We may not think we're worthy,
But he's just glad we came.

When we're looking for a friend who cares,

The one who knows our name,
He's been waiting for our hand in his,
And he's just glad we came.

When we come with our inadequate praise,
His glory to proclaim,
And angels do a better job,
He's just glad we came.

When in distress we come to God
And his salvation claim,
He takes our groans and makes them sweet,
And he's just glad we came.

So if you're unsure and hesitant
To call upon his name,
Do not delay, come to him now,
He'll be glad you came.

The Wisdom of a Butterfly

Say the word "butterfly" and a particular image comes to my mind, one of freedom, fleeting color, beauty, and grace. For me, the butterfly is a fit representation of wondrous transformation, dreams come true, and fearlessness within fragility. And like most things of nature, a butterfly is an apt if unlikely teacher, possessing characteristics worthy of emulation. He inspires me to not be afraid of change, to persevere through times of isolation and stagnancy, and to never let my dreams die. When I see a butterfly, I fly with him in my mind; he stops me in my tracks, and for a moment I see not only his beauty but the beauty in myself.

A butterfly glides on his papery wings,
Flitting from flower to flower,
Happily sipping the sweet honey dew,
He marks not the time or the hour.

After struggling out of a silky cocoon,
He takes time to let his wings dry,
Then without hesitation, dives into the air,
And soars right up into the sky.

He doesn't bemoan the short little life
That a butterfly's destined to live,
He doesn't try hard to keep to himself
The beauty he's able to give.

He simply lives moment to moment his life,
And content to just be his best self,
He blesses us all with a beauty that's rare,
A beauty that's found nowhere else.

Fragile but fearless, beautiful, brave,
He lives life so effortlessly,
I'd like to be more like a bright butterfly,
And bring beauty to all around me.

Transformation

Another of my "older" poems, this one from 1986 addresses a common misconception, one that I struggled with as far back as high school. I am referring to the fallacy that humans can make themselves be good if we just try hard enough or exert enough willpower. All those years ago, just like now, I wanted to be a better person, more unselfish, more steadfast, more loving, more giving. So I tried. I gritted my teeth and gave my very best. Maybe it worked for a day or two, maybe more, but ultimately I was not successful. Now I realize that goodness is a gift, perfection is a process, and transformation is essential. No matter how hard a caterpillar tries to be a butterfly, the only way he can become something beautiful is by surrendering to the transformation process. For humans, this holy process of change is accomplished entirely by the power of God. Only through his work in us will we become comfortable with what we see in the mirror, because in place of ourselves will be the image of him.

When I look at myself,
At this person who's me,
I always find things
That I don't want to see.

"I wish I was perfect,"
I think with a sigh,
And I make up my mind
That I'll just have to try.

So I try to be "good,"
To never complain,
To love others first
Without thought for my gain.

To always be thankful,
Trusting him with the fight,
And not go to pieces
When things don't go right.

But it just never works,
I alone can't succeed,
In being the person
I've wanted to be.

Only Jesus can change me,
I've found that it's true,
Because nothing inside me
Can make me like new.

It's the power he gives
If I'll just let him in,
That will transform this me,
And make miracles begin.

What We Choose to See

THIS WORLD PROVIDES A veritable smorgasbord of constant choices. Every day, all day, we are bombarded. And one of the most important decisions we make moment by moment is what we choose to see. I don't mean literally what we choose to look at, but what we choose to focus on and to identify with. We cannot control much of what happens to us, but we can control how we interpret and experience our world. The path to joy and success lies in what we choose to see. I choose to see the good, the positive, and the beautiful. I choose to see the angels. And I choose to always keep God's goodness and love and interest in me foremost in my line of sight. What will you choose to see?

As each day's sun rises, and we greet the bright dawn,
There's a feast for our eyes everywhere,
And our eyes take it in, whether gloomy or bright,
Whether lovely, or ugly, or fair.

But we do have a choice, to a greater extent,
Of what we will turn from or see,
A choice that it seems can begin in our thoughts,
A choice that we have, you and me.

We may gaze on the storm that we find that we're in,
As it rumbles and crashes and roars,
Or we might see the silver that lines those dark clouds,
And the outline ahead of the shore.

We might see God's hand weighing heavily down
On us and the whole world around,
Or we might see his purpose, protection, and love,
And tell those we know what we've found.

We can dwell on the evil that seems to abound,
And people who don't seem to care,
Or we might in our mind's eye see clearly revealed
The angels that walk everywhere.

The shadow that sin has brought to the earth,
Can haunt us and bring us to tears,
Or the startling beauty that still nature holds,
Can draw us to God through the years.

So what will you choose to see in this life?
And on what will you focus your eyes?
If you choose to see all the good all around you,
You will most surely show yourself wise.

A World without Trees

FEW THINGS ARE AS SUPREMELY elegant as a tree. No matter the variety, each stately trunk adorned with branches fascinates in form, color, texture, and aroma. How easy to take these giant plants for granted with their abundance throughout both cities and the countryside, standing like faithful sentries watching over the landscape. How different and bare our world would be without trees! God in his wisdom covered much of nature with bark and leaves, enriching and beautifying the outdoors as only he can. The next time you are outside, take time to stop and study a tree, reveling in the unique beauty and offering thanks for such a gift.

Imagine a world without trees,
Without their branches reaching up tall,
Imagine no bright leaves of green,
Or of yellow and red in the fall.

The trees add so much to the landscape —
Imagine the hills plain and bare,
And evergreens absent in winter,
No beautiful scent in the air.

Where would the birds have for nesting?
Where would the squirrels build their homes?
Trees are their wonderful dwellings,
Their leafy tops forming a dome.

The light wouldn't have them to sift through,
Their leaves making shadows around,
As the wind gently sways them and moves them,
Causing sunlight to dance on the ground.

Breathing would surely be harder,
Without the trees cleansing the air,
And pumping pure oxygen outward —
Trees do this with nary a care.

The sound of the wind in the treetops,
Whether roaring or whispering low,
I'd miss this sound ever so soothing,
When walking I sometimes go.

God made us so much at creation,
And in nature these wonders we see,
But one of the best gifts he gave us,
Is this marvelous thing called a tree.

The Fight of My Life

After riding in an ambulance with my husband to the ER, I was staying with him in the local hospital. He had suffered an esophageal tear that occurred as a result of severe vomiting and had been admitted for further evaluation. The hospital was so crowded that there were no more rooms available, so my husband and I were crammed with several other patients and their families into a makeshift ward. The beds were separated by curtains, and I had only a straight-backed chair to sleep on. Worried and exhausted, I spent most of that night awake and writing. My experience there in that lonely hospital is a testament to how goodness and creativity can be born out of hardship and fear, a testament to God's power during troubling times. God comforted me that night and also gave me something to share.

The fight of my life's not for breath or for beat,
It's for coolness and calmness when life brings the heat.
It's keeping afloat in the waters of doubt,
It's keeping my faith when life turns inside out.

The fight of my life's not for fame or success,
It's remembering that our dear Savior knows best.
As I walk close to him every day on this earth,
As I marvel at how God gives my soul great worth.

The fight of my life's not for poise or perfection,
It's using the Compass to find the direction

He wants me to go, whether valley or crest,
Always knowing my journey for me is a test.

The fight of my life really needn't be hard,
The battle belongs to my Shield and my Guard.
The battle seems long, but it's actually not,
When left to the one who will see that it's fought.

In the Quiet of the Morning

A RINGING ALARM CLOCK; hurried bathing, dressing and eating; and a rush for the door can make morning a time that many people dread. Those with families to rally often find mornings even more challenging. Yet morning comes every day, like a soldier marching along, whether you are ready or not. It's easy to miss the magic. How can you break free from a harsh arrival of another day? The secret is to give yourself something to look forward to. Give yourself the gift each morning of time — 15-30 minutes dedicated to seeking God by meditating, praying, reading something uplifting, or even journaling. These few minutes of sleep will not be missed. The quiet time will invigorate and center you, allowing you to tackle your day ahead with a little more grace and a lot more peace. And you won't live your day alone, but rather with your hand in God's guiding hand and your faith firmly grounded in him.

In the quiet of the morning,
Before the rush begins,
I pause for just a moment,
To take a look within.

Some days my heart is breaking,
Some days it's full of joy,
Some days I feel I'm reeling,
Though all my will's employed

To keep myself together,
And not fall in despair,
That gruesome pit that sucks you in
And leaves your heart stripped bare.

I'll take this time, these seconds few,
To seek the Lord above,
Like a drowning man needs oxygen,
I so desperately need his love.

I need new faith, I need new grace
That only he can give,
I need the Guide of Heaven,
To show me how to live.

A life in him, a life of joy,
No matter what days bring,
I'll lay hold of his promises,
And songs of praise I'll sing.

And then go forth into this day,
Expectant, waiting to see,
His way, his hand, and all he'll bring,
And all he'll make of me.

Patience

PATIENCE IS THAT MARVELOUS quality that makes us strong under duress, even when waves beat against our little craft and threaten to capsize it. Oh, to have more patience! To not falter even after day upon day, maybe year upon year, of dealing with a challenge that is beyond our control. Fortunately we can control some things — our attitudes, thoughts, and determination to never give up hope. Patience can only come to us from God but also grows the more we use it. As we study in the school of life, challenges are both our teachers and our tests, and whether we pass or fail depends largely on our use of God's gift to us of patience.

Patience is hard to practice in life,
When the trials come swiftly and long,
When your heart weighs down heavy, just like a stone,
And everything seems to go wrong.

But patience can serve as a powerful force,
To combat all Satan can bring,
Patience can firmly and steadily guide —
It's truly a wonderful thing.

Patience takes practice, that much is true,
More skill will come as we live out
Our days here on earth, for the challenges rise
In a pattern we know all about.

And our God has promised what we know is true,
That with each temptation he'll give,
Just enough patience to help us get through —
In victory we'll grow and live.

Patience is hard to practice in life,
But oh, what deep peace it can bring,
As we stretch forth our hands for whatever life holds,
Our hearts can continue to sing.

Sunlight through the Trees

So many aspects of nature provide us with feelings of peace, joy, and gratitude. Walking in a quiet woods or beside the thundering surf; watching birds and wildlife; gazing at the varied and beautiful sky. More importantly, nature turns our minds toward God, just as he intended. I enjoy so many facets of the Book of Nature that it is hard to pick a favorite. As I reclined on my couch at home, looking out the window one sunny morning, this poem came to my mind.

There's beauty all around us
When we go to the outdoors,
The flowers and the wildlife
And the shady forest floor.

But one thing that's a favorite,
That I love to often see,
Is the magic that the light makes
When it's sifted through the trees.

I hear the muted whispers
Of the wind so soft and low,
I smell the rain's aroma
When it falls to earth below.

There's lofty mountain grandeur,
There's the warm and gentle breeze,

But nothing stirs my heart quite like
The sunlight through the trees.

How it dapples! How it dances!
How it flickers makes me smile,
I could gaze at it for hours;
It bewitches all the while.

The earth is full of wonders
From the heavens to the seas,
I love it all, but so enjoy
The sunlight through the trees.

The Cat

I FIERCELY LOVE MY three cats, each with a different little personality and respective quirks. My youngest cat, Sally, is hilariously playful and engaging with eyes that shine bright with intelligence. She seeks me out throughout the day to see if I am available to serve as her sleeping surface, to dispense treats, or to turn on a faucet for her to drink. Susannah is extremely timid, shying away at times from a loving hand, but then jumping on my stomach or chest to knead and snuggle. She likes to lick my hands, arms, and face when she is feeling brave and comfortable, and she becomes very "talkative" at times. And then there's Sophie, crazy for my husband and preferring men in general. She is the most social, vocal, and demanding of the felines and also quite neurotic in her own way. These creatures are members of my family and dear to my heart. How different life would be without them, marked by an emptiness that only they can fill. Many centuries ago back in the garden of Eden, God must have known how much I would need their affection and companionship.

The cat is a clever creation,
And surely God knew from the start,
How the cat would charm and beguile me,
And steal its way into my heart.

Take for instance the cat's purr,
A sound so lovely and grand,
Its starts up not unlike a motor,

With only the touch of my hand.

The cat is a wonder to look at,
The image of beauty and grace,
From the tip of its question mark-shaped tail,
To the whiskers on its noble face.

Playful and smart is this species,
Their antics like a graceful dance,
From leaping and chasing and stalking —
The poor mouse just hasn't a chance.

A friendship so rare and so precious,
Can often be formed with a cat,
A comforting, fur-covered presence,
Who just wants to be where you're at.

I'm so glad that at the creation,
When animals to where Adam sat,
Were brought to be named, that included,
Was one that he wisely named "cat."

What Can I Say about Christmas

The timeless theme of Christmas never loses its wonder for me. I embrace everything about this joyous season — the music, the lights, the giving of gifts. Still, when I sat down to write a poem about Christmas, I didn't know where to start. I felt that anything I wrote would just be repetitive noise. Yet I persisted, not allowing myself to be put off by doubts. I realized that the Christmas story deserves repeating! We can never say or write or sing enough to reach the end of this defining celebration. The gift of our Savior elicits endless praise to God that will ring throughout eternity.

What can I say about Christmas,
That hasn't been said before?
What can I add 'bout that bright blessed night,
When Mary so humbly bore

Our Saviour, Christ Jesus, in a dirty barn
'neath a sky in which angels sang?
What would I give to have been there that night?
To have heard when their sweet voices rang

Out in the dark to men blinded with glory
And thrilled with the news that they heard?
What can I sing that hasn't been sung?
How can I add one lone word?

It boggles my mind, and makes my heart wonder

At a God who would risk all to send,
The one he loved most, then who so gladly came,
He gave all our sad world to mend.

So now every year we are blessed to remember
His birth here so many years past,
The lights in the dark, the smiles, and the music
Are all ways to make Christmas last

Through cold, dark December
And into the year, that comes ever boldly and bright,
Maybe Christmas can even last all the year long —
That spirit of goodness and light.

So what can I say about Christmas,
That hasn't been said before?
Probably nothing — yet here I am with my praise —
The Father and his Son to adore.

The Answer to Someone's Prayer

MY CAREER HAS TAKEN some crazy twists and turns. With a degree in education, plus a licensed practical nurse certification, I've worked as a public and private school teacher, homeschool teacher, caregiver, activities director, and nurse. I've stayed with jobs as briefly as two months and as long as five years. Looking back at my employment history, I struggle with feelings of regret and failure. At the same time, I know God directs my every step and has placed me in each position for a reason. In all of my places of employment, I not only learn more about myself but also touch the lives of students, patients, clients, residents, and co-workers. Mulling all of this over one day, it struck me that I could have been an answer to someone's prayer somewhere along the way. I might have been in the right place at just the right time to unknowingly be the response to a struggling soul's silent cry to God. If I have uplifted one person with concern and compassion, I have found success in heaven's eyes.

You can show someone your smile,
Say a kindly word or two,
You can brighten someone's day —
It's an easy thing to do.

You can lend a helping hand,
And lighten someone's load,
Someone who is discouraged
And whose faith is all but cold.

He may have asked the Lord,
For love and care today,
Just a signal of God's grace,
As he journeyed on his way.

He may feel down and out,
And wish someone would care,
He may feel so alone,
No one with whom to share

His thoughts and doubts and fears —
He needs another human being,
It surely would be pleasing
To our God, who's always seeing

Us as we go about,
Our jobs, our work, our play,
Let's take time to be the answer,
To someone's prayer today.